THOUGHTS
FEELINGS
TEARS

KENNETH H. WEIKUM

Order this book online at www.trafford.com
or email orders@trafford.com

Most Trafford titles are also available at major online book retailers.

Editing by Ellen Mott.

Cover illustration by Kenneth H. Weikum

Interior photos:
Mountain pictures by Joyce Abernathy.
Western pictures donated by Linda Biscarner, Ruth James, Ellen Mott and Christine Weikum.
All other pictures from the personal album of the author.

Print information available on the last page.

ISBN: 978-1-5539-5211-4 (sc)

Trafford rev. 03/01/2019

North America & international
toll-free: 1 888 232 4444 (USA & Canada)
fax: 812 355 4082

THIS BOOK IS DEDICATED

TO

The memory of **DORORTHY R. HERNIGLE**
Loving Mother of 11 Children

TO

LOUISE M. WEIKUM
Mother of Five

TO

CAROLINE(Carrie) HERNIGLE & FRANCES NABAK
My daughter's namesakes

AND TO

All those Mothers that give up so much to
love and raise their children in
this uncertain world

3

Table of Contents

Introduction

Years ago when I was sharing some of my poems with friends, a young lady asked me, "Is this what you actually think or just words that you write because they go good together?" The answer was to become the title to this book. These are my personal "THOUGHTS" about the places and people that have touched my life. My "FEELINGS" about those I've loved and was fortunate enough to have had them grace me with their love. And of the "TEARS" we all must cry throughout our lives, and some I still do. I share these with you, a total stranger, not so much that you may know me better. But with hopes that you may get to know yourself better. That they might bring reflections on your own life, so that you might fully appreciate those around you and with hopes they bring an understanding of how precious life really is and how fragile love can be.

Kenneth H. Weikum

Thoughts

Once I was young, just wild and free
Full of dreams of things I might be.
And now that time has made me old
All there is, are some stories told,
Of many fantasies and Loves gone by,
That leaves me here, waiting to die.
Now death, I'm told, is not that bad?
But it seems to make some people sad,
Yet, after all since time begin,
On this life's race one can not win.
The only difference in the sands of time
Are the footprints, we leave behind.
So if I've touched some lives with grace
And made their world a better place,
Then, when my life is finally done
I've cheated death; I've really won.

I'll never call you Darling

Friends are forever and lovers only part
So I'll never call you darling and you'll never break
my heart
But I'll always love you forever and a day.
We'll be only friends there's just no other way.
I've another woman and you've another man
So we'll be only friends, won't you please understand?
Friends are forever and lovers only part
So I'll never call you darling and you'll never break
my heart.
Now we'll never lie though a dark summer night
But we can walk hand in hand in the quiet moonlight.
There will be no need for lying, cheating, or a tear
If you never call me darling and I never call you
dear.
Because friends are forever and lovers only part
So I'll never call you darling and you'll never break
my heart.

14

Now it's hard to stay just friends and feel the way I
do
But my heart is too fragile to say; "I love you."
You set my soul on fire but it will just have to burn.
It took too many lovers but I finally did learn,
That friends are forever and lovers only part
So I'll never call you darling and you'll never break
my heart.
Yes, I'll never call you darling and you'll never call
me dear
But I'll be your friend forever and a year.
For friends are forever and lovers only part
So I'll never call you darling and you'll never break
my heart.

15

MY 55 CHEVY & SHARON T.
LEFT BOTH IN DENVER, COLO.
AND JOINED THE NAVY 1966

Ken (Tiger)
Along with the
picture I am sending
all my love to
the very one I
love so dearly.
God Bless you
Love Always
Sharon (Kitten)

Mile High

The Mile High I don't call home and never will
But a part of me is left there still
And memories of you float across my mind,
About young love and a much sweeter time.
Yes, the Mile High can be lonely and sad
With thoughts of a love that wasn't that bad.
Things happened I could not handle back then
And I lost a love I didn't win.
You sometimes lose at love's crazy game
But there will never be another love quite the same.
That Mile High I don't call home and never will
But part of me is left there still
Underneath the sky and stars so bright
In amongst the mountains tucked so tight
Those thoughts of you will also be there
And the tender love you and I did share
I can go back but never stay for long
But each visit brings memories like this song.
Yes, the Mile High I don't call home and never will
But part of me is left there still.

First Love

The first love that you have
It can never really be bad
But it cannot ever last.
That is what makes it a little sad.
Those sweet, gentle feelings,
The first time anywhere,
Will teach you to love
And your heart you will share.
You will have learned love
In a sweet and gentle way,
Thoughts of that love
With you they will always stay.
But when that love is gone,
You and your lover have parted;
Like a desert empty and bare
That love will leave your heart.
Your life will not end

And the flowers they will grow.
In your life there will be
Other loves that you know.
None so innocent, sweet, and kind
As that first love you left behind.
Now you've gotten married
Time has had to have past;
You have a family and another love.
These will always last.
Still the memory is there
And it makes you kind of sad;
That first love of yours
That is not really bad.

Haunting Memories
(A Letter From The Past)

Memories haunting my dreams ever after, I think of you night and day.

Knowing out love is a failure, it's over, and you are going away.

Think of the love that we shared in the evening, knowing tomorrow that it only would end.

This is the memory of my love, my wanting. These are the memories that will come to an end.

I love you, I want you, I need you, my Darling. Okay, what will become of this?

Is it invain to love only dreamers who wander the world in search of an end?

Will you come back or will it be over and will we see each other again?

Yes, this is the memory, the haunting, the dreaming that must all come to an end.

I love you, I love you, I love you, my Darling, oh, please don't go away.

At least send me letters to let me remember the things like they are today.

For only a moment I want you to leave for I know dreamers are made that way, to wander. But my love gets in the way.

So please forgive me for being possessive and trying to keep you only for me.

For I know you must go now and I must accept it that's what must be.

Good-bye Love
Anonymous

USS ANDREW JACKSON
SSBN 619

21

Sweet Love

Oh love, sweet love
It's been so long
Since I wrote a poem
Or even a song
You stir hidden feelings
Deep down inside
But only for a moment
Then they must hide.
It is a shame and a pity
I'll never know your heart
But life and time will
Always keep us apart.
If Heaven's angels would
Grant my one wish,

Someday I would feel
You're sweet, tender kiss
But that is impossible
So I'll sit and dream
Enjoying your beauty,
Like a clear mountain stream.
I can stay forever
Watching your smile.
It warms my soul for a country mile.
But if too soon
I say good-bye
It is because I need to be alone,
When I cry!

24

My Eyes

My eyes are fortunate for what they have seen
On a cold frosty morning, a warm sunbeam.
The sun setting on a wide open sea,
An eagle sitting high in a tree,
High Mountain peaks in a blanket of white,
A shooting star in the dark of night,
A bright red rose fresh with morning dew,
But never real beauty until they saw you.
Moonlight reflecting off your soft bare skin
Makes all the rest seem almost dim.
Yes, my eyes are fortunate, that is true
Mainly because they've seen you!!!!!!

Lost Love

The clear mountain stream
Just flowing along
Brings memories of you
And an old love song.
Under the bridge
Too much water did go.
What ever happened
I never will know.
Such lovers were we
Sharing each other's heart
Till something went wrong
And we grew apart.
That last cold night
You left without a word
Leaving me here alone
26

On love's barren ground
Yes, empty and lonely
All broken and in pain
My search for love
Had all been in vain?
Now memories of you
Drift into my dreams
Slowly and gently like
A clear mountain stream.
Yes, all that is left
Are memories and a dream.
They'll always be there
Like that clear mountain stream.

LIKE THE MOUNTAINS LIFE
MUST CHANGE WITH THE
SEASONS

5 above

High in the mountains all covered with snow
Far, Far away that's where I must go.
Because it's warmer up there when it's 5 above,
Than it is down here without any love.
Without even asking I gave you my heart
You took it, used it, an tore it apart.
Away from the lies and stories untrue
Up in the mountains away from you.
Because it's warmer up there when it's 5 above,
Thank it is down here without any love.
Yes, I'm gonna get there if it takes all year,
Where the birds and animals can share each tear
And the cold, cold wind that blows each day
Will chase all my hurt and heartache away.
Because it's warmer up there when it's 5 above,
Than it is down here without any love.
I'll be there until I'm old and I'm gray,
Up n those mountains is where I'll stay.
The snow and ice will cover my bones
And the winds will sing how I died all alone.
Because it's warmer up here when it's 5 above,
Than it I down there without any love.
Yes, it's warmer up here when it's 5 above,
Than it is down there without-
Your sweet love.

29

Kenneth-
A little extra saying
To say good bye for
Now. We'll see you
Soon again - in about
Six or eight weeks
Love
Sister Sharon

30

Navy Man

Put silver sails upon your
Chest
Make yourself one of America's
Best
Feel on your face, the ocean's
Spray,
At all times come night or
Day.
There'll be a prayer in every
Port,
But always just one girl you'll
Court.
Put her name upon your heart,
As she has yours and you'll never
Part.
And remember, too, your
Family,
They'll stand by you along with
Me.
So love your life and make it
Strong,
Make it just and good and
Long.
God please keep you safe from
Harm,
For all of us, give him a charm of
Love.
Sharon Weikum

Why Me?

As the last glimmer of light leaves the sky at sunset you can just make out the round shape of the moon. It seems to be hanging there, just above the clouds and the fog. As darkness sets in it disappears, too. The air is heavy with moisture, cool and hard to breathe. It's chilly but not cold. The fog moves in across the water and seems to draw me to the water's edge. The water is black like the night sky and only once in awhile can you see a glimmer of light from the distant shore. As the waves lap at the rocks of the shoreline, I can feel their presence. And just for an instant my soul leaves my body to dance across the water with those who have gone before me. We dance together around the same question with never an answer. Who are these souls whom I visit on a cool, foggy night?

First there was Judy's sister's baby. When I was in high school, the site of such an innocent child lying in such a small coffin, I did not understand. I didn't understand the mother's pain, Judy's pain, or why a child barely a day old would be taken from this world. Only later would I understand that God loved it so much that he would spare this child the pain of life.

Then there were my virgins. I've only been with three and we'll only talk about two now. The third will come later. The sad part is I can't remember their names. No matter how hard I try. I can remember the face of the first, the night in the front seat of a '65 Impala, but not her name. It was less than a year later I was told she took her own life, never did find out why. And number two; I can remember the couch and the color of the carpet. I still remember how soft she was to touch and the tears on her cheeks. I did not love her and why she chose me, I'll never know. Two short weeks later she died in a car accident with her family.

There were friends who did not return from Vietnam and fellow sailors that went down with their submarines. Had my orders been just a little different I might have been with them

And "Happy Grandpappy", a fellow trucker I had coffee with and a short two hours later he was killed in a truck-train accident. A Peru, Ill. Driver, here today and gone tomorrow. And a very nice lady driver from St. Louis. When going through Kansas City, a family in a station wagon lost it on the ice. She swerved to miss them and was killed when the truck rolled. Same old question, why are all these good people gone and I still survive?

More recently, there was Melvin. At a truck stop in La., he was working on the sign and got against the power lines. I still remember his lifeless body on the concrete. Mike gave him mouth to mouth and I did CPR. His hot clothes burned my foot through my boots but we got him breathing and heart working. Kept him alive until the paramedics arrived. Felt good about that and myself until I got back to the terminal. There they told me he had died. I find myself still a little angry with him.

And then there's Becky. I had a hand in killing her, you know. Should have listened closer that night. We were at her house, a couple of drivers and girls. She expressed concern about here husband being violent. We left and the next morning he came home, shot and killed her, and him. She was dead before I could even finish my trip. I've always felt I should have or could have done something.

There are others but none that affected me like the first and the last. It's good to dance across the water with them. Letting them know they are not forgotten and they give me comfort.

My soul returns to my body having their permission to live on. No real answers, just comfort in my loneliness. As I stand there staring out across the black water a breeze comes along. It blows the fog against my cheeks and the moisture collects there. I know it's their tears, can't be mine. For that's the really sad part, I've never cried over them, just over you.

33

GROWING UP

IN THE 1950s

Interstate Song

That diesel hums as we drive along,
All those trucks sing the Interstate Song.
Four days late before we even start,
We are on our way to break another heart.
That cute little waitress at the old cafe
Gonna be sad when we drive away.
Jump in that truck and grab another gear,
We don't have time to shed a tear.
Caught overloaded on our way to L. A.,
Now we are late going the other way.
Thirteenth gear is moving this old truck,
Smokey's waiting that's my kind of luck.
Make the same old stop we did yesterday.

This time that waitress isn't gonna stay.
Yes siree, she's coming along,
Gonna help me sing that Interstate Song.
All the way to Detroit, she jammed those gears.
Now we've been together almost five years.
Home for just a little while, then we're gone
Out there sing that Interstate Song.
The boss just called, we're another day late,
Better get on moving, hauling that freight.
That diesel hums as we drive along
All those trucks sing the Interstate Song.
Yes, all those trucks sing that Interstate Song

37

38

Waiting on tables

I've been waiting on tables fourteen years
Met a lot of boys, shed a lot of tears.
Couldn't meet anyone I could love true.
Didn't that is, until I met you.
You were the best, a real good man
Hoped we'd marry, put a ring on my hand.
Gave you my heart, soul, and body bare
Then you were gone, just left me there
Took my love, threw it in the trash
Just like yesterday's scrambled eggs and hash.
So now I'm waiting tables just like before
And like always, swear there'll be no more
We're closing now so I'll lock the door
Grab the mop and I'll clean the floor
Don't need any water; there's plenty of tears
After waiting on tables these fourteen years.

Lady Trucker

That lady driver behind the big wheel
One hand on the CB and nerves of steel.
Her handle's Big Rose or Little Firefly
You can tell by the voice that it isn't a guy.
It's kind of surprising she's driving that rig,
She's so little and it's so big.
And if you have thoughts of laying her down
You've got a lesson coming around.
She's all business when driving that truck
So long fellow, you just out of luck.
She's out there driving in snow and ice
Enjoying every day that is sunny and nice.

When she's working she's mean and tough
Over the CB she sounds kind of rough.
But when the run's over that diesel's shut off
She's all woman, quite gentle and soft.
Off with the boots, jeans, and clean up the mess
She's going to town wearing a dress.
Tonight she'll party and do her own thing
Tomorrow, boots, jeans and that big machine.
Back on the highway with nerves of steel
That lady driver behind that big wheel
Yes, that lady driver's behind that big wheel.

41

Outlaw Saloon

The Outlaw Saloon in western Wyoming
To lose your memory, that's where I'm going.
I'll have me a party, a drink, one or two
With a little bit of luck, I'll find someone new.
That western band will be playing right soon
And the dancing will start at the Outlaw saloon.
I'll find a new love, just for one night
I'll forget about you when she holds me tight.
When she's with me your memory can't stay
She's gonna chase all my heartache away.
We'll be in love, like the dish and the spoon
Me and my new love, at the Outlaw Saloon
Another round of drinks, a glass of red wine
Tonight she's my love, just for a short time.
We'll laugh and dance to an old western tune
Tonight I'll forget you at the Outlaw Saloon.
In the morning I'll wake, it will all be the same
Lonely as hell, your memory's to blame.
Yes, I'll think of you, about love and the moon
But tonight I'll forget you at the Outlaw Saloon
Yes, tonight I'll forget you at the Outlaw Saloon

Freezing Rain

I've stood naked out in the freezing rain
Felt the wind, sleet and icy cold pain.
I've broken my arm, my back and hip.
And felt the sting of a bitch's whip.
Been tortured, tied, bit, and burned.
Forgotten more pain than one should learn.
Been blind drunk, sick, and almost dead.
Cut myself to watch my blood run red.
But nothing compares to the pain deep inside
For all the years you were not at my side.
So if you leave again, and go far away,
Naked out in the freezing rain, there I'll stay.
Until my whole body turns cold and blue
Like my world—without you.

Choices

Choices, choices, they say it must be done
But I won't, I can't, It'll hurt someone
So back to sleep, from reality I'll hide
And give the fantasy horse just one more ride.
Too soon morning comes and with a big spin
It throws me back into reality again.
To a world where I can't (won't) stay,
So I go to hide in a place far, far away
Deep In My soul to a place I call home.
Just me alone where your memory does roam.
No choices made here but just one lie
And here I'll be until it's time to die.
Not before Gods time because that's bad.
He'll make the choice, when I'm no longer sad.
Soon I hope, please not too many years,
I've already cried way too many tears

A Purple Rose

A purple rose so rare and hard to find
Just like love we've left behind.
Maybe a dream or just a fantasy, not true
Or could it be real, this one's love for you?
But like the rose's petals, sweet and too soon gone,
Passion is short and life's way too long.
So little faith, way too many fears,
And all those doubts that caused all those tears.
Life is unfair and times the one to blame.
We cannot go back, it could never be the same.
So a piece of me is gone forever now,
I can't replace it, I don't know how.
Yet a purple rose will put you in mind
And I will feel the pain, yes, one more time.

My Sweetie

My Sweetie's a cowboy man
The best there is in this land.
When he comes to me, that hat on his head,
I'm going to heaven; he's taking me to bed.
He'll kiss me, caress me, and my body he'll hold
And with his love I'll never grow old.
My Sweetie's a cowboy man
The best there is in this land.
When he touches me and I look in his eyes,
I'm so happy that he's my guy
With his love and tender care;
My heart I'll be happy to share.
Yes, my Sweetie's a cowboy man
The best there is in this land.
In this room our love we'll show
But it's a secret no one will know

48

And whether it's right or wrong,
My love for him will always be strong.
My Sweetie's a cowboy man
The best there is in this land.
Under the moon or by the firelight
I want to love him all through the night.
But he's got to go, he can't stay long
And I'll still love him when he's gone.
Yes, my Sweetie's a cowboy man
The best there is in this land.
It's sad but true,
I'll never share his life
Because my Sweetie has a wife.
My Sweetie's a cowboy man
The best there is in this land.

When Sleep Won't Come

In the dark of the night when sleep won't come
You enter my thoughts and I hold you some.
I taste your lips, feel your soft, warm skin
As your essence fills my emptiness within.
And though my mind knows this is not reality
My heart still gets lost in this fantasy.
So, in the dark of the night when sleep won't come
You enter my thoughts and I hold you some.
We dance real close throughout the night
And we're still together come morning's light.
Then I must put these thoughts of you away
And face the reality of just one more day.
Still, in the dark of night when sleep won't come
You enter my thoughts and I hold you some
Yes, in the dark of the night when sleep won't come

50

Waiting for Forever

Been no songs or poems from the heart
Since the day we were forced to part.
Yet your memory sweetly haunts my mind,
As my soul searches for a peace it can't find.
Yes, part of me is gone forever now.
I can't replace it, I don't know how.
How could a love so right be so wrong?
But I'll forget you, when forever is gone.
For now, asleep I cry myself awake.
And wonder, how long forever will take.
At times the wait is more than I can stand
And though I'm not alone, I die a lonely man!

Bad Day

Loneliness seems to be dragging me down to its endless depths.
I'm so exhausted!
I don't have the strength to fight off the rats of reality as they gnaw
at my flesh.
I have not even enough energy to seek shelter in a fantasy.
The water draws me to its edge but I dare not go dancing through
the fog
I fear I would get lost and not be able to find my way back.
The reality of time eats away at my body as loneliness consumes
my soul.
As the shadows grow long my world turns dark and cold.
The only warmth is a ray of sunshine just out of reach.
To reach it seems almost impossible, still I must try!
Reality is cruel and the depths of loneliness are deep and I'm so
Exhausted.
So not today, okay.
Maybe tomorrow I'll have the energy and strength to try,
One more time!

Bad Day To Night

A bad day, all week, turned to night
Because someone turned out the light.
Someone new for you, I'm really glad.
But darn, it makes me oh so sad.
Now there is no hope for us or we.
Guess that's how life was meant to be.
I want you happy so I must hide
All the feelings I have deep inside.
Choices I made cause this pain I feel,
A wound that even time cannot heal.
So at your wedding I'll wish you well
And there I must say a final farewell,
Then fade to a memory where I belong.
And I'll forget you when forever's gone
Now out in the freezing rain I go to stay.
Just waiting for forever to come someday.
Yes, a bad day all week, turned to night
Because some stranger turned out my light!

A Moment in My World
(A Letter Unsent)

Come take a walk with me to a private place that very few know about. It is not too far, we won't be long, just a moment or two and nobody will even know we're gone. Just hold my hand as we step off the sidewalk and into the grass. In just a few steps we're on a path winding through the trees. Not far down the path, the grass turns brown and the trees are big, thick and barren of leaves. Some are charred black from the flames of hurt and pain. The undergrowth is nothing but thick thorn bushes made up of lies and deceit. There's not much light here because a thick cloud of doubt hangs over the trees, creating a fog and making it hard to find the path. You must find your own way, for if I show you it would be impossible for you to find the way back. It's scary but don't be afraid, I'll be right here with you.
A few steps and a couple of turns later we are out of the dark forest and standing on hard clay ground, nothing grows here. It's only about ten feet across to a twelve feet high wall made of stone and jagged rock. I built it myself one stone at a time. On top there are steel spikes to keep anyone from climbing over. The only way for you to enter is through the steel gate in front of

you. I know as you glanced up and down the wall, you noticed a small door with a light above it far down to the right. Your key will not open the door. Your way in is the main gate. It is thick, locked with heavy chain and several big heavy locks. I've added one every time someone enters then leaves. I have no keys and can not open the gate for you. As you approach the gate, you lay your hands on it to see how solid it is. When you do, the chains and locks crumble to dust. The gate seems to just gently swing open for you. I've always wondered how you did that, I'm amazed at the power your gentle, loving touch has.

As we walk through the gate you will notice the grass is rich green. The sun is shining and there are no clouds. The sun is not hot but it warms you through and through. We are standing on a path that leads across the meadow, by a horse pasture and down to the garden. On the other side of the garden there is a footbridge, the path crosses on it's way up to the house. The house is big, not huge but it has many rooms and two stories. As we walk down the path towards the horses, to the right you'll see a path from the small door. It leads from the wall to a cottage. The cottage has a porch swing and only one window.

You'll also notice, there is no path from the cottage to the house. This I must explain! I have a visitor who comes here once in awhile. She has a key to the small door and the cottage so she can come here anytime she wants. Sometimes she comes when she is hurting and other times I think she comes to check on me. Her world is different than mine and the cottage is as far as she comes. Mainly we sit on the swing and visit about each other's world. In the evening I'll tuck her in, give her a quick kiss on the cheek and return to the house alone. On rare occasions, when she's been hurt and in pain or the loneliness of the house gets too much for me, we spend the night comforting each other. But when the dawn breaks she always goes back to her world leaving by the small door. I go back to mine and the emptiness of the house. Because of our different worlds there will never be a path from the cottage to the house for her. But she always has a safe haven to come to in the cottage. She will always be a friend.

Now lets continue our walk along the path to the house, to the left is the horse pasture. A three-rail white fence surrounds it. There is a black stallion and a small Appaloosa mare. The black is wild and cannot be ridden. Yet, as you approach the fence, he comes right

to you and puts his head against your chest so you can
scratch his ears. The mare walks up and just lays her
head on your shoulder. The only time they've done that
was the last time you were here. You just seem to have
a way with things in my world. Now come with me down
the path to the garden. There is a swing in the middle
where you can sit and I'll push you for awhile. It's pretty
and peaceful here. Lilacs, Cherry Blossoms, Roses and
many other flowers and trees, we can sit here for hours
just enjoying each other's company.
As we leave the garden and head toward the footbridge,
we pass by the Roses, They're soft and come in all
colors, different shades of red, yellow, peach, and even
purple. You will notice that there are not thorns on the
roses except the purple ones towards the back. Kneel
down, inhale their sweet aroma, touch their softness but
be careful of the thorns on the purple ones.
When you are ready we'll continue our walk. The
footbridge is wood and weathered but sturdy and safe.
It crosses a creek running from a small pond. The water
here is clear and warm. You probably don't remember
but we swam together in the pond the last time you were
here. As you look down from the bridge into the water,

you can see your reflection. Your hair is blowing gently in the breeze, your eyes are soft, your face is smooth and your lips are flushed and moist. Your skin, from your toes across your tummy, your breasts and shoulders, is smooth and soft. You say that is not you, but it is. You see, the reflection here is not what other people believe or what the rest of the world sees. It is the reflection of the real you that I can see, sometimes not even what you yourself see. I see a soft, tender, loving woman, who maybe the world has made tough on the outside but she is still a beautiful person on the inside. I can see that person.

As we cross the bridge and start up the steps to the porch, you will see two dogs. They are Dobermans with slick black coats. The one on the left is the smaller of the two. I call her Fear. She is gentle but will bite. The one on the right is big and mean.   I call him Anger and he can be vicious. I know they are my dogs and sometimes I cannot control them but don't be afraid. Sit and call them to you. Pet them, run your hand across their backs, they will not hurt you today or ever again.

58

As we walk through the front door, the entryway is large.
It has a hardwood floor and no rugs. To the left is a
room with nothing in it but an old army blanket on the
floor, nothing on the walls and no furniture. Straight
ahead is a stairway to the second floor, the master
bedroom is up there with several other rooms, I think.
You see, in all the years I've kept this place, I've never
been upstairs. To the right is a small den with a
fireplace against the wall. Across from the fireplace is a
small couch with a small table on either side. One table
has a chess set and the other a submarine model. On
the wall above the fireplace are paintings of the Rocky
Mountains and a herd of BigHorn Sheep. On the floor
next to the fireplace is a bottle of wine and two glasses.
It has never been opened. In fact, nothing has changed
in this room since the last time you were here. You
never got to see this room then and it was my fault.
You see, when you were here last time, we had just
finished swimming in the pond. I gave you a towel and

59

left you to dry off, I went into the house to check and make sure everything was just right. I left the door open behind me, when I turned around you were right there behind me. You had moved so quickly from the pond into the house, you never saw the dogs. I was so startled to find you there, you raised your hand to gently touch my cheek and reassure me of your love. It startled the dogs and they attacked you. I grabbed for them and by the time I got them under control, you had fled. You ran out the door, across the bridge, through the garden, past the horses, and out the gate. I ran after you but you had reached the gate and disappeared before I could reach you. The forest was dark and full of thorn bushes. I could not find the path you had taken. Clouds of doubt settled in, blocking my vision and I could not find my way. I went back into my world, shut and locked the gate. It was a long, lonely walk down the path to the house. The horses were gone from the pasture, there were no flowers in the garden.

60

As I crossed the bridge I could not see my reflection, the water was cold and murky. When I entered the house only then did I realize how badly the dogs had hurt you. There was blood everywhere, the walls, the door, and pools of it on the floor. The dogs were cowering in the corner, heads down and very sad eves. They knew they had done wrong. But it was not their fault, they were only trying to protect me. They did not know you raised your hand to gently touch me. I knelt with my knees in the blood, coaxed them to me, stroked their heads to comfort them. Only then did I realize they had gotten me, too. There was a gash on my arm and the flesh had been torn from the bones of my fingers. I didn't think I would ever stop the bleeding. It took a long time to clean the blood up. My hand never did heal right. If I bump it wrong or someone grabs it to tightly, it starts to bleed again.
The dogs and I went looking for you several times, We could not find you and had all but given up. A

couple of others have come here since you left. One even made it to the footbridge but the dogs would not let her across. You are the only one they let come to the house. They chase all the others away. I had given up and had gathered all the stones to cover the gate. The dogs talked me into leaving and looking for you one more time. Anger stayed to guard the house and Fear came with me. We didn't think you would want to come back and visit, but we did want to check and make sure your wounds had healed better than mine had. It was only by chance that we found you on the sidewalk today and we know you have to go back to your world but we do thank you for coming to visit one more time.

I told you I'd only keep you for a moment and it may seem longer than that but it has been just a quick moment in life's time. It is time for you to leave now. Night has fallen and there is a chill in the air. Take my sweater and put it around your shoulders, it will keep you warm. I'll walk you to the bridge and the dogs will take you from there. I really would like to walk you all the way but I've shut and locked the gate and had to walk all alone too many times. I don't think I have the strength to walk back alone this time. I'll just wait here for your return. The dogs will walk with you and guard you, you are their friend and they will not hurt you again. They will keep you safe along the path, protect you through the forest and, when you are safely back in your world, they will return here to me. They know the way, as do you. When they return we will go inside the house and lock the door. We've stayed in the room on the left ever since you've been gone, just sleeping on the blanket on the floor. But tonight the house is warmer, filled with thoughts of you and hope that you will return soon. Tonight we will stay in the den and maybe, when you return, upstairs. Tonight the dogs and I will sleep in the den. They'll curl up by the fire and I'll lay my head against the pillow on the couch. I'll listen for the door to unlock and your footsteps across the floor. How will I know it is you? That's simple, you are the only one who has a key to this place!

Money

Today a friend said we'd make a dollar or two.
Told her come here, I want to talk to you.
Let's sit at the bar and have one drink,
I'll tell you a story, then we can think.
When I was a kid, just making a buck
I could save nearly half with a little luck.
It wasn't too long and I made a whole grand.
Gosh, that was more money than I could stand
Then through the years I was making over ten.
That was more money than I could spend.
After that, it was 20, all in just one year.
Bought all the food and barely enough for a beer.
It hasn't been long since I made 30 or more.
I could barely keep the wolf away from the door.
Over 40 now I can hardly buy a shot and a coke.
Money? If I make anymore I'm gonna go broke.
So offer cash for words, my feelings they tell
And I'll tell them all, go straight to...
Well, Maybe!

To My Orchid

Like the old song says,
             About the way life goes,
I overlooked an orchid
             While searching for a rose.
I found a rose out there
             As perfect as one can be
But reality, fate and time
             Kept it just a fantasy.
Yes, the reality of time
             Kept her away from me
And left me here all alone
             On life's open sea.
So I swam to the island
             Where my orchid did grow
And she still loved me
             Why I'll never know.

A true love real strong
           And sweet as can be,
And then I finally realized,
           I'm so lucky she chose me.
Now my rose is out there
           Drifting in the wind.
But I'll never go looking
           For her again,
For my orchid loves me
           In her special way
And by her side
           Is where I will stay.

Denim Cowboy

The Denim Cowboy's a strange sort of guy
He gets drunk, he flirts. And sometimes he'll cry.
But out chasing cows or driving a truck
He's always on his own, just trusting to luck.
So beware young ladies he can be awful bold
His eyes will undress you, or so I'm told.
He'll tell a joke, a wise crack or two
Just to get a laugh or a smile from you.
But it's an old trick; I've heard him say
To chase life's troubles and sorrows away
And we'll never know what he's all about
With dreams deep inside he never lets out.
So when it's all over, said and done
He will have give life one hell of a run
But in this game there is no way to win
So let's dig the grave to put him in
This shallow place is where he'll lie
That Denim Cowboy, a strange sort of guy.

From Dusk 'till Dawn

It's been ten years since you've been gone
And I still miss you from dusk till dawn.
Can't believe I still hurt this bad,
But nothing compares to the love we had!
I miss your strength I leaned on
And I still miss you from dusk till dawn.
The sun still shines and the moon still glows
And you are missed more than I let show.
Now I know they say life must go on.
But I still miss you from dusk till dawn.
And when it's been forever since you've been gone,
I'll still miss you from dusk till dawn!

Lord Walk with Me

Oh Lord, there's so much I do not understand
So please Lord, walk with me, take my hand.
A life was sent to you that was so very young
Taken from this world before it hardly begun.
In your arms and care you've taken it to stay,
But I loved it so and I miss it every day.
Are you sure you didn't make a mistake this time?
For if you'd only asked, I'd gladly traded mine.
At times I'm so angry and really mad at you
Because I do not understand all that you do.
So walk with me, help me find some peace within
Lord, help me understand that this is not the end.
So please walk with me, hold tight to my hand
Help me through this life and things I don't understand.
And in time, with your love, I will try to see
This soul is in heaven and someday I will be.

71

I Wish I Could Sing

I wish I could sing and carry a tune
Touch your heart, make love bloom.
I'd sing you a song so you would understand
The feelings deep within this man.
The music would be sweet and pleasant to hear,
And tell of pleasure when you are near.
The words would say how my love is true
And how much I do love you.
They would tell of pleasure and warmth you bring
Into my life, of that I'd sing.
And if for some reason I must go away
You would know my love would stay.
So I may be lost but not forever gone
I'll love you forever in this song.
But I can't play or sing a single note
All I have are these words I wrote.
And from my heart and soul they come so true.
Darling, I will always love you!

74

A Child's love

Forget all your troubles
And all of your sorrow
When you're with a child
It's a brighten tomorrow.
Unlike past loves
Causing hurt and pain
Your child's love
Shall always remain
Your child's love is
More precious than gold
For unlike many others
It will never grow old.
And if some foolish love
Should break your heart
Your world shattered
And coming apart
Your child will look up
With that tender smile
And you will know
Life's been worthwhile
No matter how dark
The day begins
Your child's love
Will let the sunshine in.

75

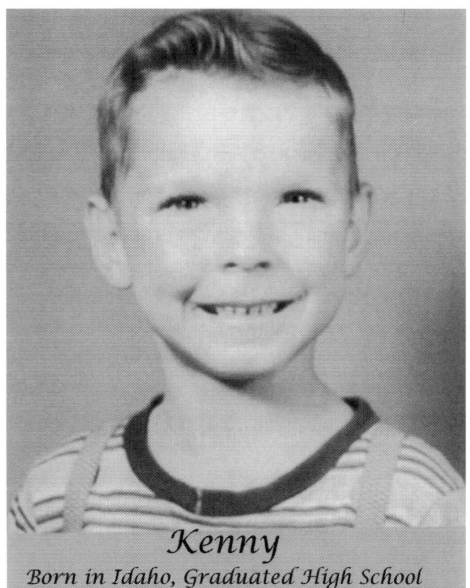

Kenny

Born in Idaho, Graduated High School
in Denver, Colo. 7 Years Navy Submarines
3 Million Miles as a Professional Driver
Not a Poet Just a Ordinary Man

A NOTE FROM THE AUTHOR

I hope you have enjoyed the book and the poems. If you would like to share it with

a friend you may order them a copy through TRAFFORD PUBLISHING.

If you would like to order individual framed copies of any of the poems you may
e-mail me at :

CFdenimcowboy@aol.com

Include your Mailing address and please use subject as
"tft poems"

I'll be happy to mail you imformation on how to order them

Thank you,

KENNETH H. WEIKUM

Printed in the United States
By Bookmasters